Snap books®

Crafts

Braiding Hair

Beyond the Basics

by Jen Jones

Capstone press®

Mankato, Minnesota

Snap Books are published by Capstone Press,
151 Good Counsel Drive, P.O. Box 669, Mankato, Minnesota 56002.
www.capstonepress.com

Library of Congress Cataloging-in-Publication Data
Jones, Jen.
    Braiding hair: beyond the basics / by Jen Jones.
    p. cm. — (Snap books. Crafts)
    Includes bibliographical references and index.
    Summary: "A do-it-yourself crafts book for children and pre-teens on braids and other
hairstyles" — Provided by publisher.
    ISBN-13: 978-1-4296-2312-4 (hardcover)
    ISBN-10: 1-4296-2312-8 (hardcover)
    1. Braids (Hairdressing) — Juvenile literature. I. Title. II. Series.
TT975.J68 2009
646.7'247 — dc22   2008023566

Editor: Kathryn Clay
Designer: Juliette Peters
Photo Researcher: Marcie Spence
Photo Shoot Stylist: Sarah L. Schuette
Photo Shoot Scheduler: Marcy Morin

Photo Credits:
Capstone Press/Karon Dubke, 5, 8 (all), 9 (all), 10, 12 (top), 14 (top), 16, 17 (all), 18, 19 (all), 20, 21 (all), 22
(right), 24 (top); Capstone Press/TJ Thoraldson Digital Photography, 6, 7 (all), 11 (all), 12 (steps), 13 (steps),
14 (steps), 15 (all), 23 (all), 24 (steps); 25 (all); Getty Images Inc./Vince Bucci, 29 (right); Getty Images Inc./
WireImage/Archive 1/Steve Granitz, 29 (left); iStockphoto/Mikhail Kondrashov, 30; Photodisc, 3, 13, 22
(flowers); Shutterstock/Jason Stitt, 27 (left); stockxpert/ginaellen, 27 (right)

The Capstone Press Photo Studio thanks Wanda Morsching, Jackie Graham, and Amy Muehlenhardt
for their braiding skills.

1 2 3 4 5 6 14 13 12 11 10 09

Table of Contents

CHAPTER 1

Tressed to Impress

Braids are like a great pair of jeans.
They can be worn just about anywhere.
From soccer games to the red carpet, braids
are designed to suit every outfit and occasion.
And it's easy to see why. Braids can add
eye-catching elegance or fun to any look.
Plus, they're easy to do.

In this book, you'll get the step-by-step
scoop on creating a variety of braids. You'll
also score hair care tips and style suggestions.
Get ready for a braiding blast!

CHAPTER 2

Before you Braid

Tress TLC

Want to say good-bye to bad hair days? Taking care of your hair is important when trying out different styles. Use the following tips and tricks for healthy, no-hassle braids:

• Tangle-free tresses are a must for successful braiding. Be sure to condition and comb out your hair before styling.

• For girls with short or layered locks, many stylists recommend working with wet hair. Wet hair is easier to manage and keep in place.

• Be careful not to pull your hair too tightly. Doing so can lead to headaches or damaged hair.

Tress Toolbox

Before braiding, you'll want the following must-have materials on hand:

· comb
· bobby pins
· coated elastic ponytail holders
· hairspray
· styling products like gel and mousse (optional)
· decorative accessories like ribbons, jeweled or beaded bobby pins, colorful clips, or even fresh flowers (optional)

Different styling products can definitely come in handy. For a smoother braid, apply mousse or gel from roots to ends while your hair is still wet. Add smoothing serum to the end of a braid for a beautiful finishing touch.

7

Braiding Basics

When it comes to braids, the sky's the limit. From braided updos to complex weaves, there are many sassy styles to learn. Before trying more advanced styles, it's important to master the basic braid. After all, the basic braid is the building block for all braid styles.

2 Cross the right section over the middle section. Move the right section to your left hand. The middle section becomes the new right section and is held in your right hand.

3 Cross the left section over the new middle section, and grab it with your right hand.

Basic Braid

1 Use a comb to separate your hair into three equal sections.

4 Repeat steps 2 and 3 until all the hair is braided. Use a ponytail holder to fasten the end.

Style for Miles

In the next chapter, you'll learn about the most common and easy-to-create braids. The fun part is that there are lots of ways to wear even the simplest braid. Here are some ideas to get you started:

Half-Tail
Braid only half of your hair. Leave the rest down in cute curls or long, straight locks.

Accent
A super-thin basic braid near the face, the accent braid is a quick way to spice up your style.

Invisible
Pin the end of your braid up and under for a more polished look. This works best with Dutch or French braids.

CHAPTER 3

Simple yet Sassy: Four Easy Braids

Say Bonjour to Braids

The French are responsible for creating many beautiful things. The Eiffel Tower, the hot-air balloon, and even the Statue of Liberty are all French creations. So it's not surprising that one of the prettiest plaits is the French braid.

Classic French Braid

1 Starting above your forehead, use a comb to separate a small section of hair from the front and sides.

2 Divide this section into three pieces. Cross the piece in the right hand over the middle piece. Then cross the piece in the left hand over the new middle piece.

3 Use a comb to add another 1-inch (2.5-centimeter) section of hair to the right piece. Cross this piece over the middle.

4 Repeat step 3 with the left piece.

5 Keep adding hair to each piece and braiding until all of your hair has been included.

6 Once all the hair is added, finish with the basic braid. Use a ponytail holder to fasten the end.

finished hairstyle

11

Going Dutch

Once you're a whiz at the French braid, try switching it up with a Dutch braid. Although both braids use similar techniques, the Dutch braid weaves the strands under rather than over. Imagine a French braid turned inside out.

Dutch Braid

1 Starting just above the forehead, use a comb to separate a small section of hair from the front and sides. This section should be slightly less than a half-ponytail.

2 Divide the small section into three equal pieces.

3 Cross the hair in your right hand under the middle piece.

4 Cross the left piece under the new middle piece.

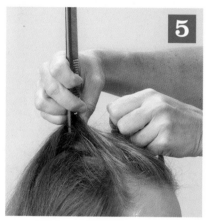

5 Use a comb to add another 1-inch (2.5-centimeter) section of hair to the right piece. Cross this piece under the middle piece. Repeat with the hair in your left hand.

6 Keep adding hair to each piece and braiding until all of the hair has been included.

finished hairstyle

7 Once all the hair is added, finish with the basic braid. Use a ponytail holder to fasten the end. Personalize the look with flowers or small hair clips.

SPRAY

13

Do the Twist

True to its name, this simple style puts a unique twist on braiding. Just like the French braid, pieces are added into the twist as you go. But unlike the French braid, only two pieces are combined to complete this look.

Twist Braid

1 Use a comb to separate your hair into two equal sections. Secure the left side with a ponytail holder so it doesn't get in the way.

2 Starting on the right side, take a section of hair near the forehead. Separate this section into two pieces. Hold one piece in each hand.

3 Cross the left piece over the right, and switch hands. The right piece should now be in your left hand. The left piece should now be in your right hand.

4 Using your right hand, add another equal section of hair to the right side. Cross it over the left piece, and switch hands again.

5 Continue steps 3 and 4 until the braid is halfway around your head. Use a ponytail holder or clip to hold it in place while working on the left side.

6 The process is the same on the left, except you start by crossing the right piece over the left. Use your left hand to add sections of hair to the bottom piece.

7 When the left twist is halfway around your head, remove the holder or clip from the right side. Fasten the two braids together with a ponytail holder.

finished hairstyle

Helpful hint: Create different looks by choosing small or large pieces to twist. Just make sure the pieces are the same size on both sides. If your hair is long enough, you can create a messy bun or a fun ponytail with the rest of your hair.

Fishing for Compliments

Want to make a big splash? This style looks hard, but it's really easy. Like the twist braid, the fishtail braid uses only two strands of hair during braiding. It's easy to get hooked on this hairdo.

Fishtail Braid

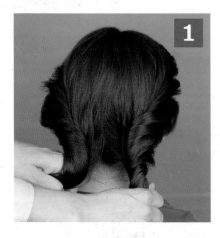

1 Use a comb to separate your hair into two equal sections. Twist the sides of each section until you reach the top of your neck.

2 Take a small piece from the outer part of the right section. Cross it over the right section to join it with the left side.

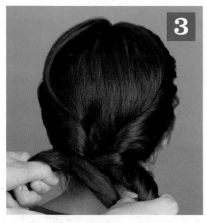

3 Repeat the process by moving a small piece from the outer left section to the right side.

4 Continue switching sides until you reach the bottom of your hair.

5 Use a ponytail holder to fasten the end.

finished hairstyle

Helpful hint: If you've done it right, your braid will look like a bunch of Vs on top of each other.

17

CHAPTER 4

Beautiful Braids for Every Occasion

Sun-Kissed Sweetie

What could be better than summer fun in the sand? A day at the beach calls for a super cute and casual hairdo. Upside-down fishtail pigtails use the same technique as the fishtail, except strands are braided under rather than over.

Upside-Down Fishtail Pigtails

1 Separate your hair into two equal sections. Then divide the right section into two equal pieces.

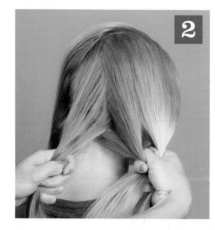

2 Take a small section from the outer part of the left piece and cross it underneath. Combine it with the right side.

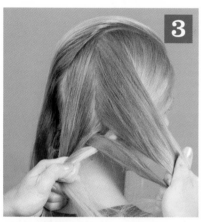

3 Repeat the process by moving an equally small section from the outer right side under. Combine it with the left side.

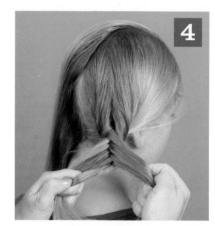

4 Continue switching sides until the braid is complete. Use a ponytail holder to fasten the end.

5 Repeat the entire process with the left section to create another braid.

6 finished hairstyle

19

The Good Sport

Ready to sweat in style? From the gymnastics mat to the soccer field, girl athletes can rock the double Dutch braid look. After all, this look allows you to run, jump, and play while your braids stay perfectly in place.

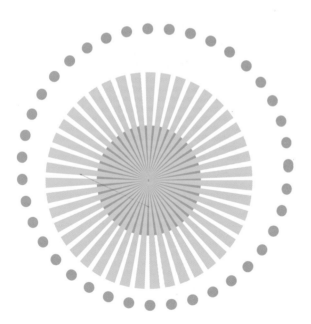

Double Dutch Braid with Ribbon

 **1** Use a comb to separate your hair into two equal sections. Secure the right side in a ponytail so it doesn't get in the way.

 **2** On the left side, take a small section of hair at the forehead and divide it into three pieces. Tie a long, thin ribbon around the top of the middle piece.

 **3** Cross the right piece under the middle piece. Then cross the left piece under the new middle piece. Make sure to braid the ribbon with the middle piece.

 **4** Continue the Dutch braid until you've added in all the hair. Finish it off with a basic braid. Use a ponytail holder to fasten the end.

 **5** Repeat steps 2 through 4 on the right side. When both braids are finished, cut off any extra ribbon or tie it in a bow.

finished hairstyle

Helpful hint: Be creative with your ribbon choices. Show your spirit with your school colors or be flashy with metallic or glittery ribbons.

Girl About Town

A great braid can be an easy way to go glam. The next time you have a formal event, let your hairstyle steal the spotlight. This fun twist on the French braid will have everyone talking about your tresses.

French Halo Half-Tail

1 Use a comb to separate your hair into three equal sections. Use a ponytail holder to hold the center section so it doesn't get in the way.

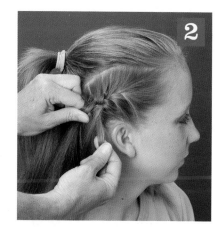

2 Create a French braid on the right side. The braid should be slightly diagonal to make a "halo" around your head.

3 Repeat step 2 on the left side.

4 Remove the center section from the ponytail holder. Tie finished braids together with a ponytail holder.

5 Use a curling iron to create loose waves with the unbraided hair.

finished hairstyle

Helpful hint: Unlike a typical French braid, these braids can be kept somewhat loose to create a softer look.

Check out any red carpet, and you're sure to see this glamorous style. Now get ready to turn a few heads of your own. With this look, you'll be the star of the show.

Braided Chignon for Long Hair

1 Make sure your hair is wet and free of tangles. For a smoother, frizz-free look, add some styling gel or spray.

2 Comb all of your hair into a high ponytail.

24

3 Create a basic braid with the ponytail. Fasten at the bottom with a ponytail holder.

4 Wrap the braid around the top holder several times until it forms a bun in back of your head.

5 Secure the end of the braid underneath with bobby pins.

6

finished hairstyle

Helpful hint: Dress up this style even more by tying a ribbon around the bun.

CHAPTER 5

Goin' Pro

With most braids, you can do them yourself or call a friend to lend a hand. But certain braid types, like cornrows and microbraids, call for the skill of a professional hairstylist.

Unlike a typical braid, these styles are worn for weeks, or even months, at a time. They take many hours of careful attention and hard work to complete, but the final results are worth it.

Cornrows (right) are a popular style adapted from African hairstyles. They consist of many raised braids created very close to the scalp. Many stylists get creative by braiding diagonals and spirals around the head.

Microbraids (left) are thin, hanging braids. Some girls use woven-in hair extensions, while others microbraid their natural hair. Though super-stylish, microbraids can also be very damaging to hair over time. Special care and conditioning is a must.

CHAPTER 6

Braiding Goes Hollywood

Braids are one of the hottest hair trends around. It's no wonder that many Hollywood celebs have taken notice.

Even celebrity guys are getting into the braided look. Soccer star David Beckham sparked a craze throughout Europe after sporting new cornrows.

Beyoncé showed off her braided chignon at a movie premier. This look is also one of Jessica Simpson's favorite styles. Her line of synthetic hair includes a braided chignon hairpiece that attaches to your hair.

Beyoncé

Alicia Keys

From concerts to the red carpet, singer Alicia Keys often sports complex designs braided into her hair.

Fun Facts

• Possibly the most famous braided hairstyle ever was worn by Carrie Fisher as Princess Leia in *Star Wars*. With her set of coiled buns, this actress brought braids to the big screen in a big way.

• Some experts think the braiding fashion trend started as early as 3500 BC. Hundreds of years later, braids are still popular hairstyles.

• Humans aren't the only ones who look great in braids. Horse manes and tails are often braided for competitions

or shows. A great-looking braid is a good way to catch a judge's eye.

Glossary

chignon (SHEEN-yon) — a smooth bun gathered near the neck

extensions (ek-STEN-shuns) — fake or real hair that is attached to your own hair to add length or volume

plait (PLAYT) — a length of hair that has been divided into sections and braided

serum (SIHR-uhm) — a styling liquid used to prevent frizz

synthetic (sin-THET-ik) — something that is manufactured or artificial rather than found in nature

Read More

Jones, Jen. *Updos: Cool Hairstyles for All Occasions.* Crafts. Mankato, Minn.: Capstone, 2009.

Neuman, Maria. *Fabulous Hair.* New York: Dorling Kindersley, 2006.

Traig, Jennifer. *Hair: Things to Make and Do.* Crafty Girl. San Francisco: Chronicle Books, 2004.

Internet Sites

FactHound offers a safe, fun way to find educator-approved Internet sites related to this book.

Here's what you do:

1. Visit *www.facthound.com*
2. Choose your grade level.
3. Begin your search.

This book's ID number is 9781429623124.

FactHound will fetch the best sites for you!

About the Author

Curly girl Jen Jones has been obsessed with hairstyles ever since she was a little girl. Although Jen didn't grow up to be a hairstylist, she is now a Los Angeles-based writer who has authored more than 30 books for Capstone Press.

Her stories have been published in magazines such as *American Cheerleader*, *Dance Spirit*, *Ohio Today*, and *Pilates Style*.

She has also written for E! Online and PBS Kids, as well as being a Web site producer for major talk shows such as *The Jenny Jones Show*, *The Sharon Osbourne Show*, and *The Larry Elder Show*.

Index